First edition 2011

Copyright © 2011 Anno Domini Publishing
www.ad-publishing.com
Text copyright © 2011 Marion Thomas
Illustrations copyright © 2011 Frank Endersby

Published in the U.S. and Canada by The Word Among Us Press
7115 Guilford Road
Frederick, Maryland 21704
www.wau.org

ISBN: 978-1-59325-191-8

Publishing Director: Annette Reynolds
Art Director: Gerald Rogers
Pre-production Manager: Krystyna Kowalska Hewitt
Production Manager: John Laister

Printed and bound in China
July 2011

The Life of Jesus of Nazareth

FOR CHILDREN

Marion Thomas and Frank Endersby

Contents

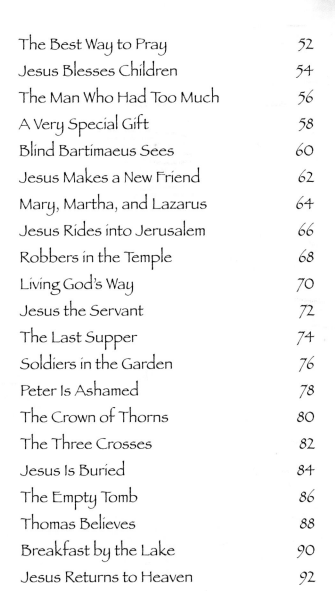

The Angel Gabriel
Luke 1:26-38

One day long ago, an angel visited a young woman named Mary to tell her something quite amazing.

"Hello, Mary," said the angel Gabriel. "God thinks you are very special." Mary was so shocked at an angel appearing in her home that she felt rather dizzy. "Don't be afraid," Gabriel went on. "This is very good news. God will bless you with a baby, and when he is born, you will name him Jesus. Everyone will be amazed at the things he does, and people will know that he is God's Son. He will be king over God's people forever."

Finally Mary found her voice. "But how can I have a baby? I don't even have a husband yet," she said.

"Nothing is impossible with God," Gabriel replied. "The Holy Spirit will make this happen. Jesus will be the Son of God himself."

Mary loved God. She trusted him.

"I am God's servant," she said.

The Journey to Bethlehem
Luke 2:1-5

Mary had been engaged to Joseph the carpenter for some time. When she told him about the angel's visit and that she was now expecting a baby, Joseph was sad. He loved Mary, but he did not think an angel had visited her—things like that just didn't happen.

Then one night the angel Gabriel spoke to Joseph in a dream. The angel convinced Joseph that such things do happen—and that he should marry Mary and take care of the baby who would be God's Son.

Months passed, and the baby grew in Mary. She became tired and

knew that soon her baby would be born. At that time,
the Roman emperor decided that he wanted to count
all the people in the lands he ruled over so that he could
tax them. Everyone had to return to the town of their ancestors
for a census.

So Mary and Joseph went to Bethlehem because Joseph was
descended from King David, who came from Bethlehem. It was a long way
for a pregnant woman to go.

No Room at the Inn
Luke 2:6-7

There was noise and bustle everywhere when Mary and Joseph arrived in Bethlehem. They were not the only visitors. There were soldiers, families, and animals, and more people looking for somewhere to stay than there were places to put them.

Joseph found a place where they could settle for the night. They shared it with the animals that were kept there. Not long afterward, the cries of a tiny new baby mixed with the sounds of the night in Bethlehem. It was Mary's baby son. She remembered what the angel Gabriel had said.

"Jesus," she whispered. "Your name is Jesus."

Mary wrapped up her baby warmly and made a bed for him in the manger filled with hay.

Some Very Frightened Shepherds
Luke 2:8-20

Shepherds watched over their sheep by night. Now, outside Bethlehem, a group of them were warming their hands and settling down for the night.

Suddenly the sky was filled with bright light, and as they fell back in fear, they heard the voice of an angel.

"Don't be afraid!" said the angel. "I have some wonderful news for you and for everyone on earth! A baby has been born today—no ordinary baby but the One you have been promised, the One you have been waiting for—your Savior. You will know him when you find him because he is wrapped in swaddling clothes and lying in a manger."

Before the shepherds had taken in his message, the angel was joined with thousands of other angels, all singing praises to God: "Glory to God in highest heaven, and peace to his people on earth!"

Then the angels left the shepherds alone, with the sound of their singing echoing in their ears.

"Well, what are we waiting for?" said one.

The shepherds found the baby lying in the manger, just as the angel had said. Then they told everyone they met about what had happened that night.

Wise Men from the East

Matthew 2:1-12

It was a starry night when Jesus was born. Wise men, far away in eastern lands, saw a new star appear in the sky. They believed that it was a sign of the birth of a new king for the Jewish people.

They packed gifts, prepared for a long journey, and traveled by night, following the star.

When the men neared Jerusalem, they went to the palace of King Herod so they could find the baby king. Herod was suspicious, and then anxious, and then angry! He didn't want another king to replace him. He thought of a way he could get rid of the baby king as soon as the men from the East discovered where he was.

"Try Bethlehem," Herod said sweetly. "But do come back and tell me when you find him so that I can worship him too."

The men followed the star to Bethlehem, where they found Jesus in a house with Mary and Joseph. They offered him their

gifts—gold, frankincense, and myrrh—and bowing low,
they worshipped him.

Mary watched thoughtfully as the men left to return
to their own country. What could all this mean?

The Escape into Egypt
Matthew 2:13-23

Joseph slept badly that night. Then he woke suddenly. An angel had warned him in a dream that Mary's son was in danger. King Herod would not rest until the child was dead.

Joseph woke Mary and together they gathered their things. They took Jesus by night on a long journey into Egypt.

Meanwhile, King Herod was furious. He knew that the men from the East must have found the child and gone back another way. In his rage, he sent soldiers to kill all the little boys in Bethlehem who were young than two.

Jesus spent his early years in Egypt. When at last Herod died, an angel told Joseph that it was safe to return to their home country. Joseph took Mary and Jesus to live in Nazareth in Galilee, and they made their home there.

Jesus in Jerusalem
Luke 2:41-52

The years passed. Each year Jesus looked forward
to the Passover and the trip to Jerusalem to
celebrate it. Families and friends traveled together
on the pilgrimage that took them from little
Nazareth to the busy, bustling city. Jesus was now
twelve, and it was that special time of year again.

Everything went well until after they had
left to return home. Mary and Joseph found
themselves a day's journey from Jerusalem—and
they couldn't find Jesus! At first, Mary thought that Jesus was with
the other children. But soon they realized that he was nowhere to be
seen. Anxiously they made their way back to Jerusalem, leaving their
friends and family behind.

Where could Jesus be? To their surprise, Mary and Joseph
found Jesus perfectly well, sitting and talking with the teachers in
the temple.

"We have been so worried!" Mary said at him. "How could you do this?"

"Why were you looking for me?" said Jesus, equally surprised. "Surely you knew I needed to be here in my Father's house?"

Mary and Joseph looked at each other and shook their heads. They didn't understand what he had meant. Jesus went back with them to Nazareth. But Mary quietly stored all this in her heart.

John Baptizes Jesus

Luke 3:3-22

Elizabeth was one of Mary's relatives. Her son, John, had grown up around the same time as Jesus. Now John was a grown man, and he spent his time in the desert, living apart from other people. He dressed differently and ate wild honey and locusts.

John traveled from place to place, giving people a message from God.

"Repent!" John told anyone who would listen. "Tell God that you are sorry for all the bad things you have done. Ask God to forgive you, and then change your ways. Be kind to others, be generous to the poor, and be fair in everything you do."

Then John encouraged them to be baptized in the River Jordan as a sign that their sins had been washed away.

One day Jesus came to the river and asked to be baptized. John knew that Jesus had done nothing wrong. He didn't need to be baptized.

"I want to do this, John," said Jesus. "Please baptize me."

As Jesus came up out of the water, the Holy Spirit appeared above him as a dove. Everyone there heard a voice from heaven saying: "This is my Son whom I love very much. I am so pleased with him."

Time in the Desert

Luke 4:1-13

Jesus was about thirty years old. It was time for him to start the work that God wanted him to do. But first he spent some time in the desert, thinking and praying. During this time he had nothing to eat for forty days, and he was very hungry.

"If you are God's Son, turn these stones into bread to eat," said the devil.

"The Scriptures tell us that man needs more than bread to live," Jesus replied.

The devil then took Jesus to a very high place. "Worship me, and I will give you all the kingdoms of the world," he said.

"The Scriptures tell us that we should worship God and no one else," replied Jesus.

The devil then took Jesus to the top of the temple. "Throw yourself down! The Scriptures tell us that God will send angels to catch you," he said.

"The Scriptures also say that we should not put God to the test," replied Jesus.

The devil knew who Jesus was—and he had tested him. But Jesus had not given in.

Fishermen Friends
Luke 5:1-11

Jesus began to tell people about how much God loved them. Many crowded around him near the Sea of Galilee, wanting to hear more.

"Can you push your boat out a little so I can talk to people from there?" Jesus asked Peter, who was washing his nets with his brother, Andrew. So Jesus talked to the people from Peter's boat. Afterward Jesus asked to be taken farther out into deeper water. "Let down your nets and do some fishing," Jesus suggested.

"I'll do it," Peter told him, "but we fished all night and caught nothing."

As soon as they cast their nets into the water, they were filled with silvery, slithering fish—so many that the nets couldn't hold them all. James and John came to help them, but the catch was so heavy that both boats started to sink. Peter looked from the fish to Jesus. He couldn't believe what had just happened!

"From now on," said Jesus, "I want you to follow me and catch men instead of fish."

Peter, Andrew, James, and John left their nets and followed Jesus.

27

A New Way to Live

Matthew 5:21-25, 38-48; 6:1-4, 25-34

28

Jesus taught his new friends—his disciples—how to follow God's ways. He explained the laws that Moses had given to the people of Israel long ago and what following them was all about.

"You know that you must not murder," Jesus said. "But it's just as bad to hate someone or wish that bad things would happen to them. Learn to love your enemies and be kind to people who hurt you. Forgive people who have been unkind to you and make peace with them.

"Give generously to anyone who needs your help, but do it quietly and secretly. Treat other people kindly—think about what you would want, and do that for them.

"And don't worry so much. Trust God to give you enough food to eat and clothes to wear. He cares about you even more than these birds and these flowers around you. And look at them! The birds have enough to eat, and the flowers are beautiful. Do what is right and good and kind, and God will take good care of you."

The Man Who Couldn't Walk

Luke 5:17-26

Four men had heard all about what Jesus said and did. They had a friend who could not walk or even sit up. Maybe Jesus would make him well.

So when Jesus was in Capernaum, they carried their friend on a stretcher to see him. But they were not the only people who wanted to see Jesus. Many were crowded inside a house listening to Jesus, including the teachers of the law. There was no room for the men and their friend.

The four men looked at the steps outside leading to the roof of the house. Then they carefully made their way up the steps and began to make a hole in the mud and branches of the roof. The people below stared up at them. Jesus smiled at them.

When the hole was big enough, they lowered their friend down into the room. Jesus knew they believed that he could make the man well.

"It's time to go home," Jesus said to the man. "Your sins are forgiven. Stand up and take your bed away with you."

The people gasped as the man stood up. Jesus had healed him, just as his friends had hoped. But the teachers of the law frowned and shook their heads. They thought, "Only God can forgive sins!"

The Soldier Who Believed
Matthew 8:5-13

Some people feared the Romans who lived in their towns. Others hated them. But in Capernaum there was a Roman soldier who loved God. He had paid for the synagogue to be built in Capernaum. He was in charge of many men. People liked and respected him.

One day he came to Jesus. There was something wrong.

"Please," he said to Jesus, "I need your help. My servant is ill and in terrible pain."

"Of course," replied Jesus. "I will come right away and heal him."

"There's no need," said the soldier. "You don't have to come all the way to my house. Just say the word, and I know he will be healed. I command many men, and they do as I tell them. It's the same for you—speak and it will be done."

Jesus turned to his friends, surprised.

"There are many people here who love God and have known him since they were children—but even they do not have such faith. I have never met anyone who trusts God as this man does."

Then Jesus told the soldier that his servant was healed. When the soldier returned to his house, he found his servant well again, just as Jesus had promised.

Who Is Jesus?

Luke 8:22-25

Jesus was tired. He had been surrounded by people all day long, and many had gone away happy and healed from their illnesses. Now Jesus needed some time to rest. So he said to his disciples, "Let's go to the other side of the lake."

They climbed in, and his friends started to sail the boat. Within minutes, Jesus was asleep.

Suddenly clouds covered the sun, and from nowhere a storm blew up over the lake. Choppy waves pushed the fishing boat around, and water gushed into it.

"Master! Help us or we'll drown!" they shouted.

Jesus woke up and saw the frightened faces of his friends.

"Peace. Be still," he said to the wind and the waves.

Almost as suddenly as it had started, the storm died down. Soon the waves were once more gentle ripples on the water.

The men looked at each other, amazed. Who could this be? Who was their friend, the man who had spoken to the wind and waves and calmed a storm?

Jairus' Little Girl

Luke 8:40-55

Jesus was met by a crowd when he came back across the lake. Jairus, the synagogue leader, made his way through the people, looking very anxious.

"Please come quickly!" he said to Jesus. "It's my little girl. She's dying!"

Jesus followed Jairus as fast as the crowd would allow. But suddenly Jesus stopped.

"Who touched me?" he asked, looking around him.

There were people all around. Surely they were all touching him! But a woman came forward, her eyes cast down.

"It was me," she whispered. "I knew if I could just touch your cloak, I would be healed."

"Go in peace," said Jesus. "You are healed because you trusted me."

But it was too late for Jairus' little girl. A man came from his house to say that she had already died. But Jesus would not listen. "Don't be afraid," he said to Jairus. "Believe, and she will be saved." Then he went into Jairus' house with Peter, James, and John.

"Get up, little girl," Jesus said to her. The girl opened her eyes and smiled at her parents. "I think she's hungry," Jesus said. Her parents cried with happiness. Jesus had healed their little girl!

Food for a Hungry Crowd
John 6:1-13

All day long Jesus had been teaching the people about God and healing those who were sick. They were far from the towns and villages.

Then Jesus asked his disciples where they could buy bread so the crowd wouldn't go home hungry. Philip could hardly believe what Jesus had asked. There were more than five thousand people there! But Andrew came forward with a young boy.

"This boy has offered us five pieces of bread and two little fish," he said to Jesus. "But it won't go very far!"

"Don't worry," Jesus said as he smiled at the boy and took the food. "Now, let's get everyone to sit down on the grass."

Jesus thanked God for the food and broke the bread and fish into pieces so it could be shared. Everyone shared with everyone else. Everyone had enough to eat—and twelve baskets full of leftovers were collected! The people knew that what had happened was a miracle. Jesus had provided food for thousands of people—with only a boy's packed lunch!

Jesus Heals a Deaf Man

Mark 7:31-37

As people heard about all the things that Jesus did, they looked for him, hoping he would help them too.

One day some people brought a man to Jesus who could not hear, and because he could not hear, he had never learned to speak.

"Please, can you help him?" they asked Jesus. "Can you make him well again?"

Jesus wanted to get away from the crowd. He took the man aside and touched his ears and tongue. Then Jesus prayed, "Be opened!"

The man looked at Jesus, and then he looked all around him, surprised. He could hear the birds singing. He could hear the sounds of the wind in the trees and the waves on the pebbles by the Sea of Galilee. He could hear the voices of his friends talking.

Jesus had healed the deaf man—and his friends couldn't stop talking about it!

The Story of the Good Samaritan
Luke 10:25-37

Jesus loved to talk about God, and people loved to listen. Sometimes they asked him questions. Often he answered them by telling a story.

"I know I must love God and my neighbor too," a man said to Jesus one day. "But tell me who my neighbor is."

"There was a man traveling on the long and lonely road from Jerusalem to Jericho," Jesus said. "Robbers jumped out and attacked him, stealing everything he had and leaving him lying on the side of the road, half dead.

"First a priest walked past him, then a Levite. Both were too busy to stop and help. They pretended they couldn't see the man who needed them.

"But the Samaritan who walked along that long and lonely road was not too busy. He stopped and gave the man water to drink. He bathed his wounds and helped him onto his donkey. Then he took him to an inn and paid for a clean bed so the man could rest there until he got better.

"'Take good care of him,' the Samaritan said to the innkeeper. 'When I come back this way, I will pay for anything else that you have spent on his care.'

"So tell me," Jesus asked the man, "who do you think was a good neighbor to the man who was hurt? When you know the answer, you need to make sure you act in the same way he did."

43

The Story of the Lost Sheep
Luke 15:3-7

All sorts of people came to listen to Jesus. Most were ordinary people. Some were the tax collectors, hated by everyone. Others did things that were wrong. Many thought that such people didn't deserve God's love.

Jesus welcomed them all. But the Pharisees and some of the religious teachers couldn't understand why Jesus wanted to be the friend of people who did bad things.

So Jesus asked them a question.

"Imagine you are a farmer who owns a hundred sheep. One day you count only ninety-nine. What would you do? Would you sit back and be happy that you still had ninety-nine sheep? Or would you be worried about the one that was lost and alone? I'll tell you what you would do! You would leave the other sheep safe in their fold and not rest until you had found the one that was lost. Then you would be so happy that you would bring him home and tell all your friends.

"Imagine what it's like for God. There is great joy in heaven over just one person who is sorry and asks God to forgive him."

The Story of the Loving Father
Luke 15:11-24

Jesus also told them another story about how much God loved people. It was about a man who had two sons.

"'Father,' said the younger son, 'I want you to give me my inheritance now, before you die. I want to travel and see the world.'

"So the father gave his son a large sum of money. He watched sadly as his son packed his bags and went away. The boy traveled and made friends. He spent his inheritance enjoying himself, and everything seemed fine—until he found that he had spent everything he had. Then a

famine swept through the country. The boy was so hungry that he had to find work. So the boy who once had so much money now had a job taking care of pigs. And he was still hungry.

"Then the boy realized how silly he was. He thought about his father and all the people who worked for him. He knew they all had plenty to eat. 'I will go home to my father,' he thought, 'and tell him how sorry I am. I don't deserve to be called his son, but perhaps he will let me work for him.'

"So the boy went home. But his father had been waiting for him all that time. He ran toward him and threw his arms around him. 'Father, I am so sorry,' he began. But the father had already forgiven him. He was already calling his servants to find clean clothes for his son and to prepare a feast for him. 'Look, my son has come back!' he told them all. 'I thought he was lost, but now he's found! Let's celebrate!'"

Treasure in Heaven

Luke 12:13-34

Jesus talked about God's love—but he also talked about money.

"It's easy to think that money can solve all your problems—but be careful! Money isn't everything, and greed can spoil your life.

"Once there was a rich farmer who had a very good harvest. His barns were overflowing, so he decided to tear them down and build bigger ones. He was very pleased with all his money and everything he owned—and he thought he could now retire and enjoy it all.

"But that night was his last on earth. He died before he could enjoy any of it. He had put all his effort into making money—but he couldn't take it with him.

"Don't make the same mistake," said Jesus. "People are more important than things. Do good deeds. Be kind and honest. If you share what you have with those who need it, it will be like storing up treasure in heaven. Then no one can steal it away and no moths can eat it. That's the way to live your life."

The Man Who Came Back

Luke 17:11-19

Most people kept their distance when they saw lepers nearby. They were afraid of the skin disease, which damaged people's fingers and toes and noses. So lepers couldn't live with their families—they had to live somewhere else. But Jesus wasn't like other people.

As he traveled toward Jerusalem, Jesus reached a village, where he saw ten men huddled together. They knew who he was.

"Jesus, please, help us if you will!"

Jesus came closer.

"Of course I will help you," he said. "Go and see your priests. You are healed. You can return to your homes."

The men were very happy when they realized that Jesus had healed them. One man, a Samaritan, came back to Jesus with a big smile on his face.

"Thank you!" the man said. "You've changed my life!"

"But where are the others?" said Jesus. "Are they not happy too? But go on your way—your faith has made you well."

The Best Way to Pray
Luke 18:9-14

Jesus often spent time talking to God. He knew God was his father. He knew God wanted to spend time with him.

"Let me tell you a story about prayer," Jesus said one day.

"Two men went into the temple. They both wanted to pray. The first man stood where everyone could see him. He prayed in a loud voice so that everyone could hear what he said. 'Thank you, Lord, that I am not greedy. Thank you that I am good and kind, honest and generous. Thank you that I am not like that man over there!'

"The other man went to a corner of the temple where no one could see him. He whispered to God so that no one else could hear him. 'Please forgive me, Lord. I am so sorry for all the bad things I have done.'

"Both men prayed," said Jesus. "God listened to both of them. But God was able to help the man who needed him and that man went away at peace. Make sure your prayers are like his. The other man only wanted to tell God how good he was."

Jesus Blesses Children

Luke 18:15-17

"Look, there's Jesus!" said a mother to her child. "Shall we go and see him?"

Other mothers followed. They all wanted Jesus to bless their children. Jesus always had time for the children, even if he was busy and even if he was tired.

Sometimes his friends tried to keep the children away. They thought he had more important things to do.

"Let the children come to me. Don't ever try to stop them," said Jesus. "God's kingdom will be filled with people like them. No one can come to my Father unless they are like these children—ready to trust him because they know he loves them."

The Man Who Had Too Much

Luke 18:18-30

People often came to Jesus and asked him questions. One time a young man who was very rich came to Jesus.

"Tell me," the man said, "what must I do to live with God in heaven?"

Jesus smiled at him. "I am sure you know all the commandments that Moses taught. You need to obey them."

"I know them," the man replied. "I have always done my best to follow them."

"Good. Now go and sell everything you have. Give the money to people who need it more than you do. Then come and join my friends. Follow me."

The young man looked surprised and upset. This wasn't the answer he had expected. He wasn't sure he could do what Jesus had asked of him. He was rich and didn't want to give away the things that mattered to him. He went away sad.

"It is easier for a camel to walk through the eye of a needle than for a rich man to enter God's kingdom," Jesus said.

"We have left everything to follow you," said Peter.

"I know," Jesus replied. "And you will all be rewarded. Put God first, and nothing else will seem important. God will make sure you have everything you need."

A Very Special Gift
Mark 14:3-11

Jesus had been invited to Simon's house for supper. The men were talking and eating together.

But then everyone became quiet as they saw a woman come into the room. She was carrying a small jar. She approached Jesus, and without saying anything, she opened the jar and poured some perfume over his head. The smell was beautiful. The perfume must have been very expensive.

Simon and his friends watched. They couldn't believe what they were seeing.

"What are you doing?" said one of Jesus' friends. "This is a terrible waste. We could have sold this perfume and given the money to the poor!"

"No, not this time," said Jesus quietly. "She has given me a very special gift. You can help the poor any time you choose. But I will not be here much longer. She has prepared my body for my burial."

Jesus knew that soon he would be taken away from his friends and arrested. But his friends did not understand what he meant. One of Jesus' twelve disciples, Judas, was particularly unhappy. He went to find the religious leaders who did not like Jesus. He was ready to betray his friend.

Blind Bartimaeus Sees

Luke 18:35-43

Bartimaeus sat by the side of the road in Jericho day after day. He felt the sun warming his skin. He heard the sound of coins being thrown into his begging bowl. He smelled the goat near him munching on vegetables. But Bartimaeus could not see.

So when Jesus came to Jericho, Bartimaeus wanted to be noticed.

"Jesus, I'm over here!" he called out as he heard a crowd approaching.

Many people wanted to talk to Jesus. Bartimaeus heard the voices of children and the sounds of many feet coming closer.

"Jesus, please help me!" he shouted again.

"Shhhh! Jesus is busy," someone said to him.

But Jesus came toward Bartimaeus and spoke to him.

"What do you want me to do for you?" asked Jesus.

"Please," begged Bartimaeus, "I want to be able to see."

Jesus smiled and said, "Receive your sight." Bartimaeus blinked hard and then broke into a wide grin. He could see the faces of the people all around him.

"Thank you! Thank you!" Bartimaeus shouted at the top of his lungs. "I can see! I can see!"

Then Bartimaeus joined the crowd of people who were following Jesus along the road.

Jesus Makes a New Friend

Luke 19:1-9

Zacchaeus was a tax collector. He was very short and very rich. The people of Jericho knew that Zacchaeus cheated them. No one liked him very much.

So when Jesus came to visit Jericho, Zacchaeus was eager to see him. He thought, "If only Jesus could be my friend!" But Zacchaeus couldn't even see Jesus over the heads of the people in front of him.

So Zacchaeus decided to climb a fig tree to get a better view of Jesus. He was just peeping through the branches when he saw the face of Jesus looking up at him! Then, in front of a crowd of people, Jesus asked Zacchaeus if he could come to his house for dinner.

Zacchaeus couldn't get down that tree fast enough.

After his meeting with Jesus, Zacchaeus was a new man. "I want to share what I have with the poor," he said. "And if anyone thinks I have cheated him, I will pay him back four times what I owe."

Jesus smiled. "This is why I am here," he said. "I came to help people who have lost their way."

Mary, Martha and Lazarus

John 11:1-46

Jesus often stayed at the home of his friends, Mary, Martha, and Lazarus, who lived in Bethany. So when he received a message telling him that Lazarus was ill, he was very sad.

But it was a few days before Jesus traveled back to Bethany to visit Lazarus. As he approached their home, Martha came out to meet him.

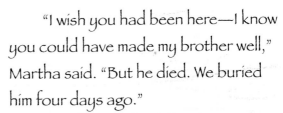

"I wish you had been here—I know you could have made my brother well," Martha said. "But he died. We buried him four days ago."

"Lazarus will live, Martha," Jesus told her. "Do you trust me?"

"I know you are God's Son," Martha told him. "I know you can do anything."

Mary was inside the house, weeping for her brother with their friends. Martha went to get her, and they all went to the tomb where Lazarus was buried. Jesus was very sad and cried with them. But he knew what he was going to do.

"Open the tomb," Jesus said. They all watched as the tomb was opened and Lazarus walked out— no longer dead but alive!

Everyone was happy to have Lazarus back with them. But they were also amazed that Jesus had healed even a dead man. Jesus really was God's Son.

Jesus Rides into Jerusalem

Matthew 21:1-11

The Passover celebration was approaching, and Jesus planned to be with his friends in Jerusalem for the special meal. He knew that this would be the very last Passover he would celebrate with his friends.

When Jesus reached a village at the Mount of Olives, he asked two of his friends to find a donkey tied up there and bring it back to him. His friends spread some of their cloaks over the donkey's back to make it more comfortable for Jesus, and he climbed on. Then he rode toward the gates of Jerusalem.

There were people lining the streets—men, women, and children. Many of them recognized Jesus.

"Here he comes—it's Jesus!"

"Did you hear he healed a blind man?"

"What about the man who couldn't walk—it's a miracle!"

"And he tells wonderful stories!"

The people waved huge palm branches and laid their cloaks down on the road before Jesus. Everyone was cheering.

"Here comes Jesus!"

"Hooray for Jesus!"

"Praise God—our King is here!"

Some people were less pleased to see the welcome Jesus received.

"Who is this man?" they said. "Who does he think he is?"

Robbers in the Temple
Luke 19:45-47

The people followed Jesus through the streets of Jerusalem. They followed him into the temple courts. Jesus was going there to pray.

It was not a quiet place. Some were selling doves and pigeons. Others were arguing over the coins they received as the money changers put them into their hands.

"What is happening here?" Jesus asked. "This is not a marketplace. It's not a place to buy and sell and cheat people! This is my Father's house, and it is a place to pray!"

Jesus tipped over one of the tables. Coins fell everywhere. Birds scattered and squawked.

"Go from here!" Jesus shouted.

The religious leaders saw what had happened. They shook their heads.

"This must stop," they said to one another. "We cannot let him stay here any longer."

"But the people love him and listen to everything he says. We cannot do anything while he is so popular."

"Then we must find a way to get rid of him. Jesus is not welcome here."

Living God's Way
Matthew 25:31-46

Over the next few days, Jesus spent time talking with the people who came to him.

"There will come a time when God will say to some of you, 'Well done! You were generous with your food and money and shared what you had with me. You took care of me when I was ill, and you visited me when I was in prison.'

"Don't be surprised! You may think that you did none of these things. But if you ever did this for someone who needed your help, then you did it for God.

"But God will say to others, 'I am disappointed with you. Why did you not share your food with me when I was hungry? How could you see me in rags when you had expensive clothes to wear? What were you doing when I was in pain? Where were you when I was lonely in prison?'

"These people will be amazed. They will deny they ever ignored him. But God will say, 'I was there with the hungry person every time you did not feed him. I waited in the hospital with the person who wanted you to visit. I was always there when you could have helped someone—and you didn't.'

"Show God that you love him," said Jesus. "Take care of other people. Be kind to anyone who needs your help. God will be there."

Jesus the Servant
John 13:1-17

For the Passover, Jesus and his disciples met together to eat supper in an upstairs room in Jerusalem.

Jesus surprised them by putting a towel around his waist so he could wash their dusty feet.

"But this is a servant's job," said Peter. "I can't let you wash my feet!"

"That's why I am doing this," Jesus replied. "I want to show you how to look after each other. This is what I want my friends to do. Take care of each other. Treat each other kindly. People will know that you are my friends because they will see that you are different. You won't think that you're too important to wash each other's feet."

When Jesus had finished, they all settled down to eat. All twelve of Jesus' disciples were there.

73

The Last Supper

Luke 22:7-34

Jesus blessed the bread and broke it into pieces. He shared it with his friends.

"This is my body, which I am giving to you." he said. "Do this to remember me."

Then Jesus blessed the cup of wine and passed it around for each of them to drink.

"This is my blood," he said. "It will be shed for you so that your sins may be forgiven."

Then Jesus said, "You are all my friends, but one of you will betray me tonight."

"I would never betray you," said Peter. "I would do anything for you!"

"Oh, Peter," Jesus said sadly, "before the cock crows

this day, you will have denied three times that you even knew me."

Judas crept out of the room during the meal. He had already decided to betray Jesus to the religious leaders. They had given him thirty pieces of silver in exchange for information about where Jesus would be that night.

Soldiers in the Garden

Luke 22:39-46, John 18:1-14

Jesus took his friends to a garden of olive trees where he liked to pray. Everyone was tired.

"Stay nearby while I pray," he asked them.

The men sat and watched for a while, but soon they fell asleep.

"Father," Jesus prayed, "I know what must happen to me. But if there is any other way, please help me now. I want to do what is right. I want to do what you want most of all, but it is so hard."

When Jesus returned, he found his friends asleep. Then he saw the lights from the torches in the moonlit

garden. Jesus knew that his time with his friends was over.

Judas led a band of men to him and greeted Jesus with a kiss. The kiss was the sign that Judas had agreed upon beforehand with the soldiers so they would know who to arrest.

Two men came forward and arrested Jesus. Then his friends panicked. Most of them ran away. But as Jesus was led away, Peter and John followed in the shadows, hoping no one would see them.

Peter Is Ashamed

Matthew 26:57-75

Peter followed Jesus and the men with swords and clubs until Jesus was taken to the high priest for questioning. It was dark and cold. Peter waited in the courtyard, warming his hands by the fire. He tried to understand what was happening. A few hours before, they had all been eating together. Now Jesus had been arrested and taken away. But what had Jesus done wrong?

"Aren't you one of Jesus' friends?" someone said to him accusingly.

"No, I don't know him," Peter said quickly.

"Yes, I'm sure you are," said another.

"No, really, I don't know him!" Peter said again.

Awhile later, just as it was beginning to get light, someone else said to Peter, "You are one of them—you sound like you're from Galilee. You have the same accent."

"I told you, I don't know Jesus!"

At that moment a cock crowed. It was morning. And Peter wept.

The Crown of Thorns

Matthew 27:11-31

The Jewish leaders took Jesus to Pontius Pilate. They wanted Jesus to be killed, and they needed the Roman governor to do it.

Pilate questioned Jesus but couldn't find him guilty of any crime. Even the Roman governor needed a reason to have someone executed.

Pilate knew that the people loved Jesus, so he took Jesus outside and showed him to the crowds.

"Look! Here is Jesus, the man that some of you call a king. I find him not guilty. But it is the custom to release a prisoner at this time of year. Shall I release Jesus? Or would you rather I release the murderer Barabbas?"

Pilate expected the people to ask for Jesus. Then he could set him free, and the religious leaders could do nothing about it. But Jesus' enemies were prepared. They had people in the crowd ready for this moment.

"Barabbas!" they shouted. "We want Barabbas!"

"But what shall I do with Jesus?" asked Pilate.

"Crucify him!" they shouted even louder. "Crucify him!"

Pilate washed his hands. He would not be guilty of this innocent man's murder.

"Take him away," he ordered the soldiers.

The soldiers put a crown made out of thorns on Jesus' head and dressed him in a purple robe. They whipped him and then led him away to be crucified.

81

The Three Crosses

John 19:17-37

Jesus carried a heavy piece of wood on his shoulder. It was the cross on which he was to be crucified. He stumbled along the street. Women and children stood along the way, weeping.

When he reached the place of execution, a hill called Golgotha, the soldiers put him on the cross between two criminals.

"I thought you were God's Son," said one. "If you are, save yourself, and us too!"

"We deserve our punishment," said the other. "He's done nothing wrong. Remember me when you get to heaven, Jesus."

"Today you will be with me in paradise," Jesus replied.

Mary, his mother, was at the foot of the cross, weeping. John, one of his disciples, was also there, comforting her.

"Look after her, John," Jesus told him. "Now she is your mother.

"This is your son now, Mother," Jesus said to Mary. "He will look after you."

Many people cried as they saw how Jesus suffered on the
cross. This was the man who had healed people, the man who
was their friend. How could this have happened?

As the hours passed, the sky grew dark.

Finally Jesus spoke one last time before he died.

"It is finished!"

A soldier stood nearby.

"He really was God's Son!" he said.

Jesus Is Buried

Matthew 27:57-61

That evening a rich man named Joseph, who came from Arimathea, went to visit Pontius Pilate. He had met Jesus and listened to what he said and taught. He had become one of Jesus' friends.

Joseph did not want Jesus' body left on the cross. He asked for permission to take it down and bury it properly in the tomb that he had prepared for his own death one day.

The Roman governor gave him permission. Joseph went with another friend and took down the body. They wrapped it in a clean linen cloth and placed it in the tomb, which had been carved out of rock. They rolled a large stone in front of the entrance of the tomb before sunset of that same day.

Mary Magdalene and some of the other women followed them to see where they had put the body of their friend.

The Empty Tomb
Luke 24:1-12

Mary Magdalene woke before dawn on Sunday morning. She gathered some herbs and spices in a basket so she could anoint Jesus' body, and went with the other women to the tomb in the garden where she had seen the men bury Jesus.

When they arrived, the first thing they saw was the large stone rolled away from the entrance. They went nearer and looked inside. The tomb was empty!

"Why are you looking here for a dead man? Don't you know that Jesus is alive!" It was the voice of an angel.

The women ran back to the town to find the disciples. They found the eleven friends and told them that the tomb was empty and that Jesus had risen from the dead.

The men did not believe them. Peter and John ran back to the tomb to see for themselves. They also saw the stone rolled away and the strips of linen that had wrapped the body still in the tomb. But Jesus was not there.

Thomas Believes
John 20:24-28

That evening the friends talked together behind locked doors about what had happened. They were still frightened that soldiers would come for them too.

Suddenly Jesus appeared in the room with them. He had not unlocked or opened the door—but he was there, and he was very much alive! He showed them the wounds in his hands and his side and talked with them for a while.

Thomas had not been there when Jesus came to the locked room.

"Unless I see Jesus for myself and touch his wounds, I just can't believe it!" he said when they told him that Jesus was really alive.

About a week later, Jesus came again to the locked room.

Thomas was amazed.

"Hello, Thomas," said Jesus. "Touch my hands. Can you believe now that I am really here?"

Thomas fell to his knees.

"It is you, Lord! I do believe."

"I am glad you can believe what you see with your own eyes," said Jesus. "But many will be blessed in the future when they believe what has happened even though they have not seen me."

Breakfast by the Lake

John 21:1-14

The disciples went back to Galilee. One night Peter asked if anyone wanted to go fishing.

Seven of the friends went out on the lake. They were out all night but caught nothing. Then, as the sun rose, they heard someone calling to them from the shore.

"Let down your nets on the other side of the boat," the man said.

The fishermen put out their nets again and caught so many fish that the nets nearly tore.

They knew who the man on the shore was.

"It's Jesus!" one of them shouted.

Peter could not wait for the boat to come to shore. He jumped into the water and waded to the beach.

Jesus was warming some bread over a small fire.

"Bring some fish so we can have breakfast," he said.

Peter still felt bad about telling people that he didn't know Jesus.

"Do you love me, Peter?" Jesus asked him three times.

"Yes." said Peter. "You know that I do!"

"I want you to look after all my friends, Peter. Take good care of them."

Jesus Returns to Heaven

Acts 1:1-11

Jesus met his friends from time to time for forty days after his resurrection. They never knew when or where they would see him. But Jesus ate with them and talked with them.

The eleven disciples and the women were not the only people to see him. Sometimes he came and talked to a whole crowd of people— people who were his friends and had followed him.

There was one more important thing he had to tell them.

"Stay in Jerusalem," he said. "Wait for the gift of the Holy Spirit to be given to you. Then God will give you the power

to tell everyone you meet about me.
Tell them how I died and about the
miracle of the resurrection. Tell everyone.
Make sure people all over the world know what
you know. I will always be there to help you."

Then Jesus left them for the last time. A cloud hid him, and he
returned to his Father in heaven. Suddenly two angels appeared.

"He has gone now," the angels said. "But he'll come back one
day, and it will be just as amazing!"